Birth and Growth

Anita Ganeri

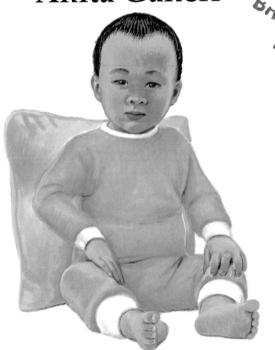

RSVP

RAINTREE
STECK-VAUGHN
PUBLISHERS
The Steck-Vaughn Company

Austin, Texas

Series Editor: Pippa Pollard
Editor: Jane Walker
Science Editor: Kim Merlino
Design: Sally Boothroyd
Project Manager and Electronic
  Production: Julie Klaus
Artwork: Cilla Eurich
Cover artwork: Cilla Eurich
Picture Research: Juliet Duff

Library of Congress
Cataloging-in-Publication Data
Ganeri, Anita, 1961–
    Birth and Growth / Anita Ganeri.
    p.   cm. — (First starts)
    Includes index.
    ISBN 0-8114-5519-X
    1. Human Growth — Juvenile
literature. [1. Growth.
2. Childbirth.]   I. Title.   II. Series.
QP84.G25 1995
612.6—dc20   94-14373
                        CIP AC

Printed and bound in the
United States by Lake Book,
Melrose Park, IL

1 2 3 4 5 6 7 8 9 0 LB 98 97 96 95 94

Contents

Where Do You Come From?

Your body is made of millions and millions of **cells**. They build your bones, skin, and all the other parts of your body. They also keep your body working. But you started life as just two tiny cells—an egg and a sperm. These joined together and grew inside your mother's **uterus** for nine months, until it was time for you to be born.

▽ We may look different, but we all started life in the same way.

The Start of Life

A baby is made from an egg cell from its mother and a **sperm** cell from its father. Egg cells are the biggest cells in the human body. Sperm cells are among the smallest. Eggs are stored in a woman's **ovaries**. Once a month an egg travels down a tube, called the **fallopian tube**, toward her uterus. Sperm are made in a man's **testes**. They travel along a tube and out through his penis.

▽ Sperm look a little bit like tadpoles. Each sperm has a head and a long, thin tail. The tail helps the sperm to swim forward.

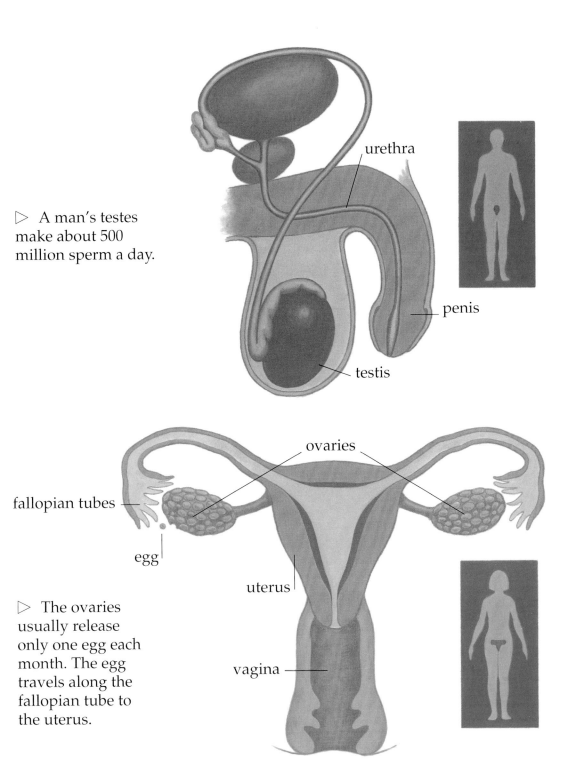

▷ A man's testes make about 500 million sperm a day.

urethra

penis

testis

ovaries

fallopian tubes

egg

uterus

vagina

▷ The ovaries usually release only one egg each month. The egg travels along the fallopian tube to the uterus.

How a Baby Begins

For a baby to grow, an egg cell must join with a sperm cell. This is **fertilization**. Sperm from the father swim up through the mother's uterus and into the fallopian tubes. If there is an egg in the tubes, the sperm swarm around it. Only one sperm can break into the egg and fertilize it. The other sperm die.

▷ Millions of sperm are made, but only one is needed to join with the egg to start a baby.

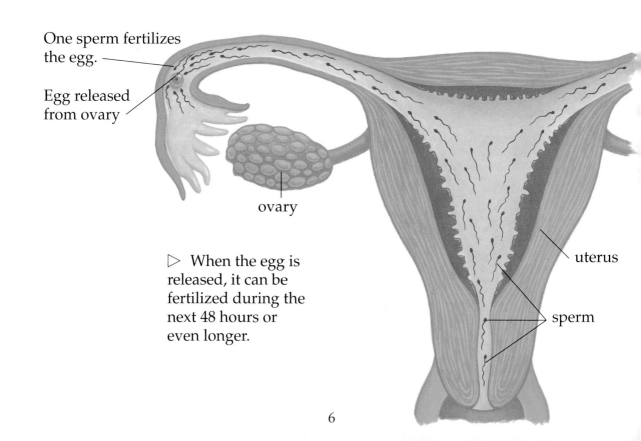

One sperm fertilizes the egg.

Egg released from ovary

ovary

▷ When the egg is released, it can be fertilized during the next 48 hours or even longer.

uterus

sperm

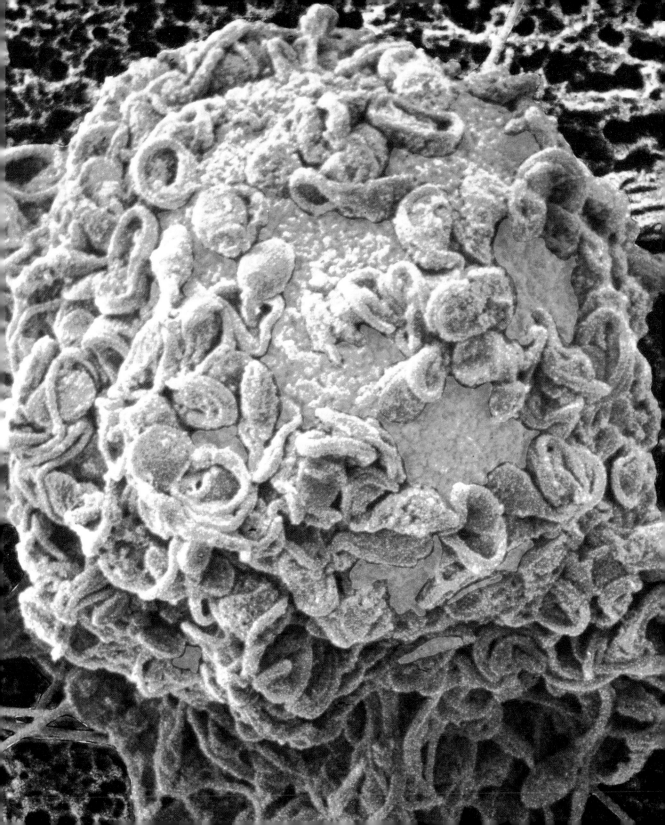

Inside the Uterus

The fertilized egg splits into two cells, then four, then eight, and so on until it forms a solid ball of cells. The **embryo** travels down the fallopian tube to the mother's uterus. It then sticks to the lining of the uterus and starts to grow. The embryo is protected inside a bag of liquid. It gets food and oxygen from its mother through an organ called the **placenta**.

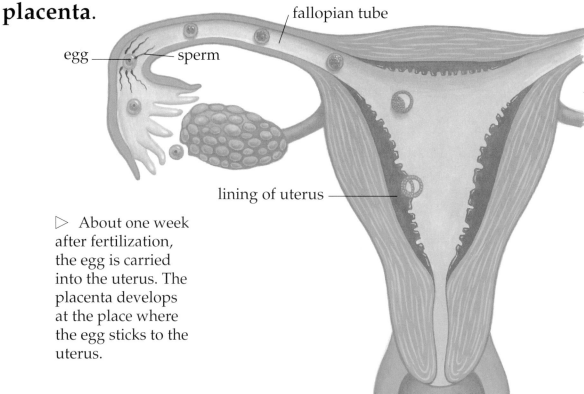

fallopian tube

egg — — sperm

lining of uterus —

▷ About one week after fertilization, the egg is carried into the uterus. The placenta develops at the place where the egg sticks to the uterus.

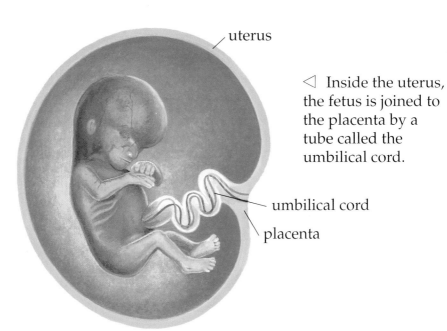

uterus

◁ Inside the uterus, the fetus is joined to the placenta by a tube called the umbilical cord.

umbilical cord

placenta

▽ Doctors and nurses use a special method called ultrasound to look at the fetus inside the uterus.

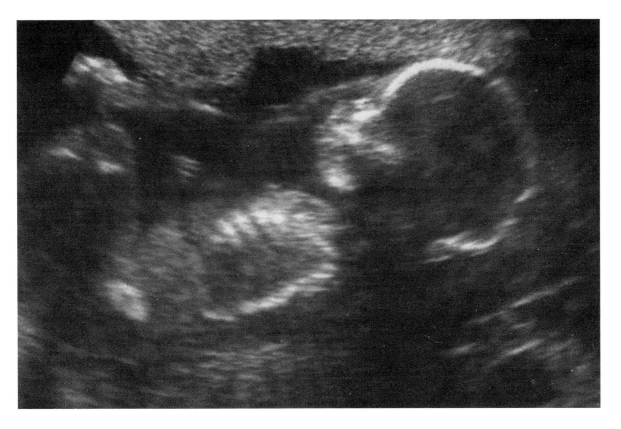

The Fetus Grows

After about two months, the baby has grown to look like a tiny human being. Now it is called a **fetus**. Its heart beats, and its body quickly grows bigger. The fetus sleeps and wakes up. It even gets hiccups. It moves around inside the uterus, sometimes kicking its mother with its legs.

▽ As the fetus grows, it stretches its mother's uterus and makes her belly bulge out.

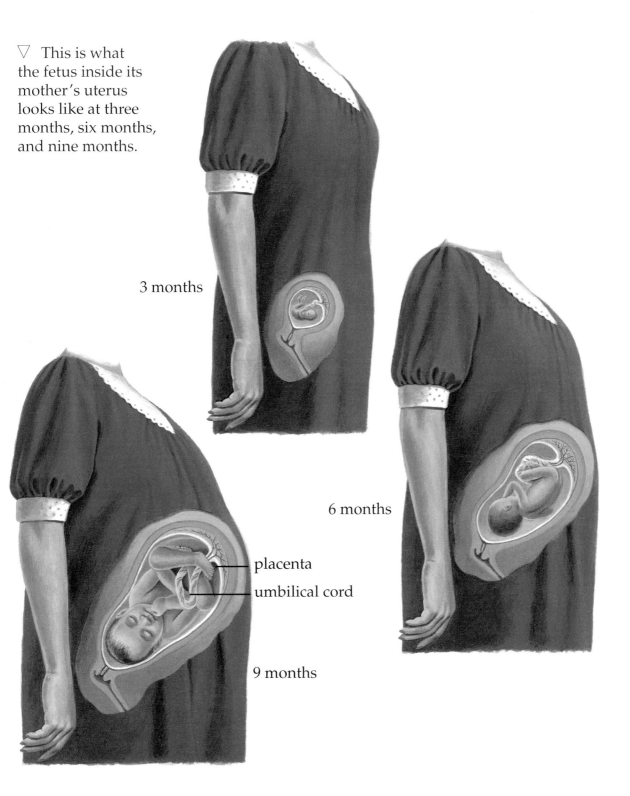

▽ This is what the fetus inside its mother's uterus looks like at three months, six months, and nine months.

3 months

6 months

placenta

umbilical cord

9 months

Being Born

After nine months, the fetus is ready to be born. It usually turns upside down, ready to squeeze out of its mother's body. The bag that protects it bursts, and the liquid pours out. The muscles of the uterus squeeze to push the fetus out through the mother's vagina. A newborn baby soon starts crying. This helps to get air into its lungs.

▷ This newborn baby has blue eyes. These may change color later. The baby cannot focus on anything at first.

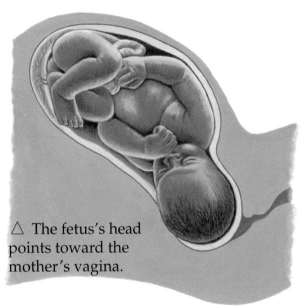

△ The fetus's head points toward the mother's vagina.

▽ Having a baby is called labor. The birth of a baby can be very tiring for the mother.

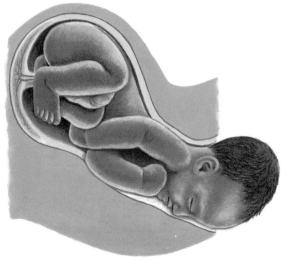

▷ The head pushes out through the vagina.

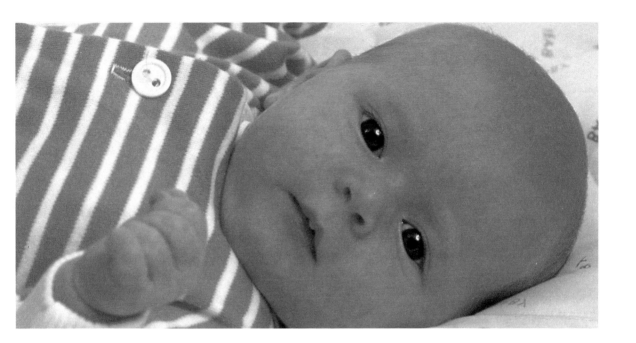

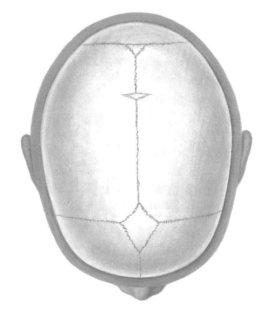

▷ The top of a baby's skull is soft and squishy so the baby's head can squeeze out of its mother more easily at birth.

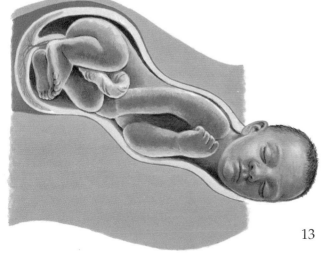

◁ The head comes out of the vagina.

Boy or Girl?

Each of your cells contains tiny threads called **chromosomes**. These contain instructions that control how you grow and what you look like. The instructions in a chromosome are called **genes**. You get half of your chromosomes from your mother and the other half from your father. That is why most children look like their parents. Two special chromosomes, called X and Y chromosomes, determine if a baby will be a boy or a girl.

▷ The genes in your chromosomes control what you will look like. For example, if both your parents have brown hair, you'll probably have the genes for brown hair.

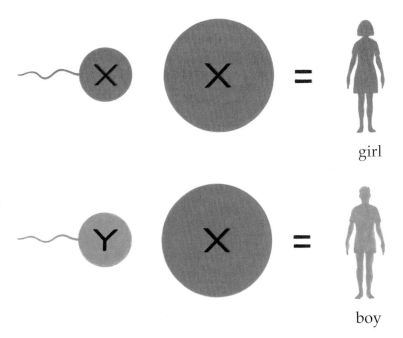

▷ Each egg has an X chromosome. Sperm carry either the X or the Y chromosome. If an egg joins with an X sperm, a girl will grow. If an egg joins with a Y sperm, the baby will be a boy.

X and X means a girl. X and Y means a boy.

girl

boy

Twins

Mothers sometimes have two babies at a time, or twins. There are two types of twins—identical and **fraternal**. Identical twins are born when a fertilized egg splits in two. Each half grows into a new baby. The twins have exactly the same genes, so they look identical. Fraternal twins are born when two eggs are fertilized. The twins have different genes and do not look the same.

▽ Identical twins are always the same sex, and they look alike.

16

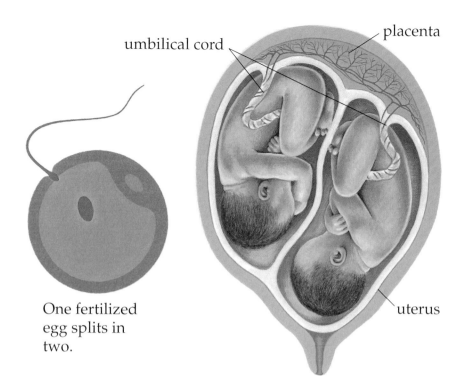

placenta

umbilical cord

▷ Identical twins share the same placenta.

One fertilized egg splits in two.

uterus

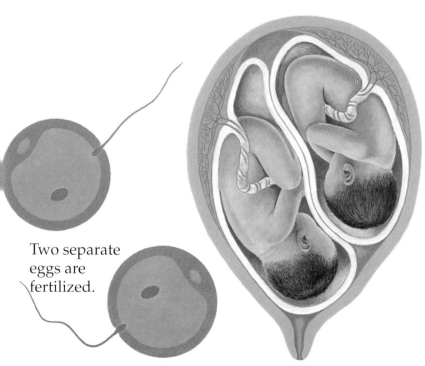

◁ Each fraternal twin has its own separate placenta.

Two separate eggs are fertilized.

Learning About Life

At first a baby does things by instinct, such as sucking and swallowing its mother's milk. This means that it does not have to think about what it is doing. But babies quickly learn about the world around them. They learn to smile, laugh, and make sounds. They also learn to control their body, so they can sit up and eventually walk on their own.

▷ Babies learn to smile when they are about six weeks old. They can laugh when they are about four months old.

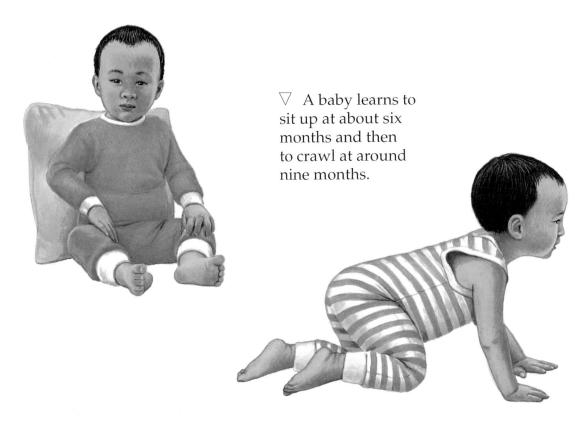

▽ A baby learns to sit up at about six months and then to crawl at around nine months.

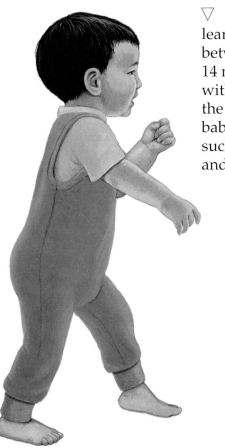

▽ Most babies
learn to walk
between 12 and
14 months. Playing
with toys is one of
the main ways a
baby learns actions
such as gripping
and pulling.

How Do You Grow?

Your body grows until you are about 18-20 years old. It gets bigger because the cells inside it divide and make new cells. There are also special chemicals inside you, called **hormones**, that make you grow. As you grow, your bones get longer, and you become taller. Your muscles get stronger, too. You grow very fast during your first two years and again when you are a teenager.

▽ Your hand has a total of 27 bones. About half the bones in your body are in your hands and feet.

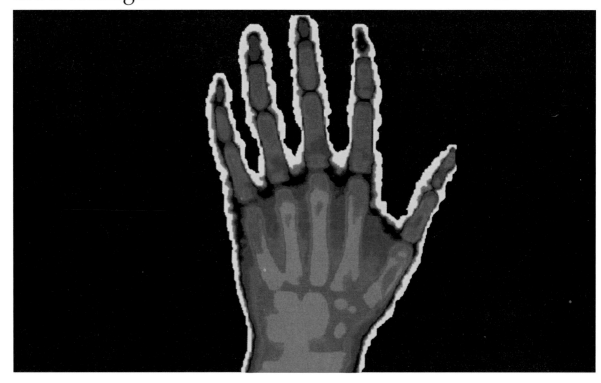

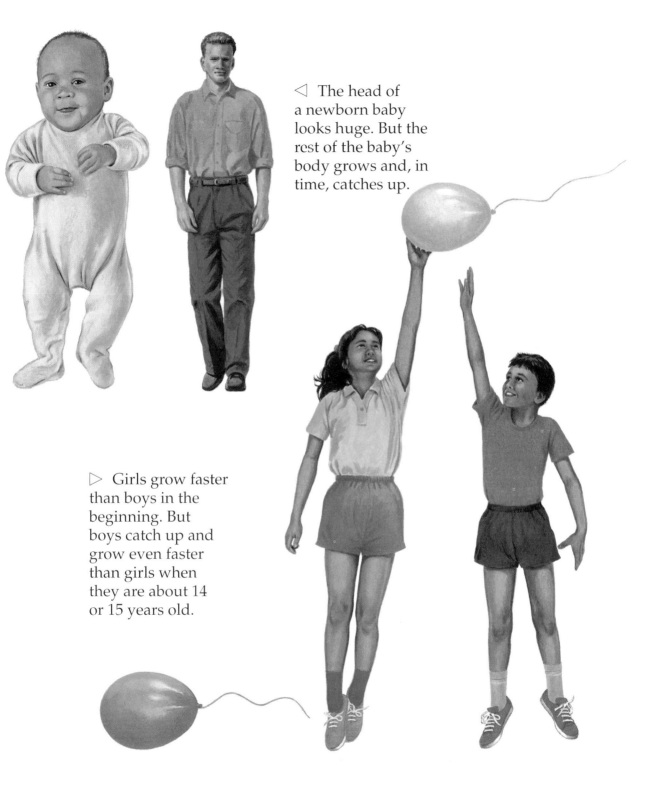

◁ The head of a newborn baby looks huge. But the rest of the baby's body grows and, in time, catches up.

▷ Girls grow faster than boys in the beginning. But boys catch up and grow even faster than girls when they are about 14 or 15 years old.

Growing Boys

Between the ages of about 11 and 18, you grow from a child into an adult. Changes happen in your body. Many of these changes are to make you ready to have children of your own one day. These changes are controlled by sex hormones, which flow around inside your blood. The hormones in boys make hair grow on their face and body, and their testes begin to make sperm.

▷ Teenage boys, as well as girls, sometimes get acne on their skin because of the hormones working inside them.

▷ As teenage boys change, both their height and weight increase. A boy's voice gets deeper, or "cracks." This happens because his voice box grows bigger.

Growing Girls

Sex hormones also work on a girl's body to prepare it for having babies. Her breasts develop, and hair grows under her arms and on her body. Her hips get wider. This is the time when her **periods** start. A small amount of blood comes out of her body every month. This happens because each month the uterus builds up a blood-rich lining for the embryo. When an egg is not fertilized, the lining breaks up and passes out of the body.

▽ A girl's body usually changes before a boy's body. These changes take place over three or four years.

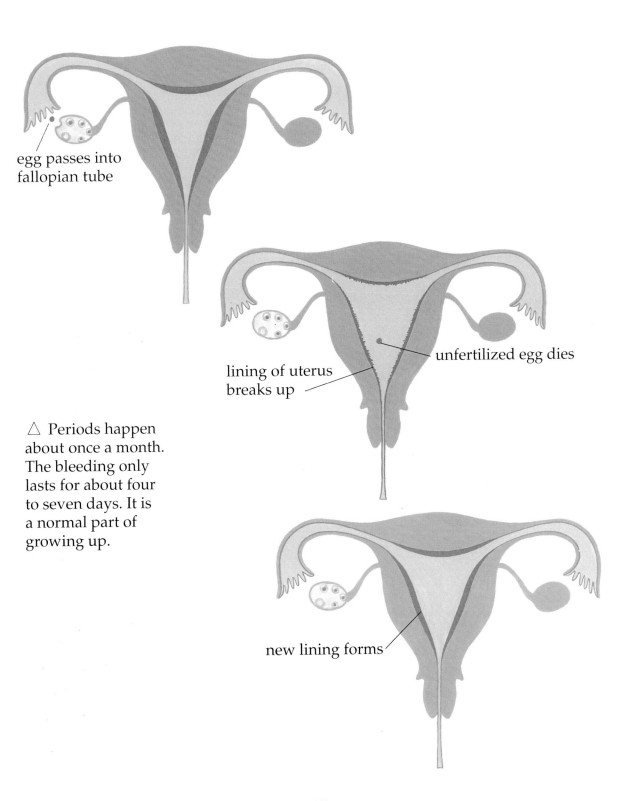

egg passes into
fallopian tube

unfertilized egg dies

lining of uterus
breaks up

△ Periods happen
about once a month.
The bleeding only
lasts for about four
to seven days. It is
a normal part of
growing up.

new lining forms

25

Adult Life

Around the age of 20 or so, you stop growing taller. You might still grow fatter if you eat too much and don't exercise enough! For the next 30 years, your body stays much the same on the outside. But inside, your cells are busy repairing and replacing old and worn-out parts. When people reach adulthood, many start to have families of their own. When people reach the age of about 40-50, they are said to be middle-aged.

▷ When a cell divides, it splits into two identical cells.

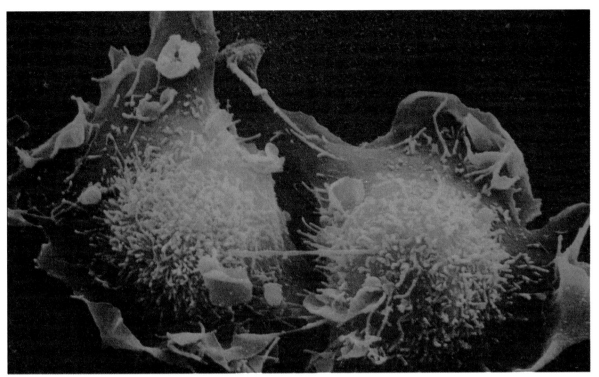

▽ How many
people are there in
your own family?
Do you have any
brothers or sisters?

Growing Old

As people get older, their bodies begin to change. They may become ill more easily because their cells cannot carry out repairs. Their skin gets wrinkled, and they may stoop when they stand up. But if people take care of themselves, eat a **balanced diet**, and keep fit, they can live for many years.

▷ On average, women live to the age of 79, and men, to 72.

▽ Many people stoop when they get older. This happens because the disks of cartilage between bones in their back shrink, making their spine shorter.

Things to Do

- People grow at different rates. Measure yourself, your sisters or brothers, and your parents on your birthday each year. How much has each person grown?

- Carry out an eye and hair survey. How many people in your class have brown eyes? How many have blue eyes? Which color of hair is the most common?

Useful Addresses:

A.A.P. (American Academy of
   Pediatrics)
Dept. C
P.O. Box 927
Elk Grove Village, IL 60009-0927
(You must include a self-addressed,
   stamped envelope.)

N.I.C.H.D.
(National Institute of Child Health
   and Human Development)
9000 Rockville Pike
Building 31, Room 2A32
Bethesda, MD 20892
(State your age.)

Glossary

balanced diet   A diet that includes a range of nourishing foods to keep you healthy.

cell   One of the millions of tiny units that make up every part of your body.

chromosome   A tiny thread inside a cell. It contains instructions (genes) that control what you look like, and whether you are a boy or a girl.

embryo   The fertilized egg. It is called an embryo from the third week until the eighth week of growth.

fetus   The young human from the end of the eighth week until it is born.

fallopian tube   A tube inside a woman's body. An egg travels down the tube on its journey toward the uterus.

fertilization   The process of an egg joining with a sperm cell.

fraternal   Fraternal twins are born at the same time but do not have the same genes.

gene   An instruction carried by a chromosome. It controls what someone will look like.

hormone   A chemical that controls changes inside your body. One type of hormone controls how fast you grow.

ovary   The part of a woman's body that stores and releases eggs.

period   A slight bleeding from a woman's body. It happens about once a month if an egg is not fertilized.

placenta   An organ that connects a mother's body with the fetus's body. Food and oxygen pass from the mother's blood through the placenta and into the fetus's blood. Waste passes out the other way.

sperm   A sex cell made by a man. It has to join with a woman's egg for a baby to grow.

testes   The parts of a man's body that make sperm cells.

umbilical cord   A cord that connects the placenta with the fetus's body. When the baby is born, the cord is cut. It leaves a mark called a belly button.

uterus   A stretchy, muscular bag inside a woman where a fetus grows. It is also called the womb.

Index

Photographic credits: Scott Camazine/Science Photo Library 20; Chris Fairclough Colour Library 3; Robert Harding Picture Library 13, 15, 19, 23, 29; T Hill 9; Francis Leroy, Biocosmos/Science Photo Library 4; Keith Parker/Science Photo Library 27; David Sharf/Science Photo Library 7; ZEFA Picture Library 10, 16, 24.